MALLY'S
little
HANDBOOK

A Guide to
Finding Your Joy
Through My Designer Eyes

Written by Mally Skok
Illustrated by Sally Murphy

This book is dedicated to

my darling children—

Paulie, Jess, and Gabrigoo!

The greatest fan club

a person could ever wish for!

Mally's little Handbook:
A Guide to Finding Your Joy Through My Designer Eyes

Illustrations and Creative Design by Sally Murphy
Copyediting by Rebecca Faith, Faith Editorial Services
Developmental Editing by Susan Baker and Judy Schenk
Closing Editing by Diane J. McDougall, McDougall Editorial
Final Templates by Allie Marshall Pesch, AMP Designs, LLC

Published by

FIREPOND
PRESS

Scottsville, Virginia, U.S.A
firepondpress@gmail.com
www.firepondpress.com

The flame and wave logo is a trademark of Firepond Press.
We are committed to coaching authors who tell stories
that inspire their readers to
"Wholeness, Boldness and Wonder."

Library of Congress Control Number: 2020923726

First Edition

ISBN: 978-0-9992204-5-0

Printed by Bang Printing, Brainerd, MN (USA); SFI® Certified
Special thanks to Brian Jansma and Jessica Ansorge

Printed in the United States of America

About Mally

Mally Skok is a Boston-based interior designer and textile maker, originally from South Africa. Following a global upbringing, Mally and her family moved in the mid-1990s from London to America, where she launched her interior design business. Mally has since built a client base that is enamored with her creative mix of layering the new with the old and transforming homes into comfortable, colourful living spaces. Mally, a tastemaker, a noticer, and a woman with a mission to empower others, has inspired her followers and design friends. She lives with her husband and two doggies outside Boston and travels to South Africa and elsewhere to visit her beloved mum and three grown children.

Contents

Preface

The bulk of this book flew off my fingertips while sitting on the squidgy sofa on our covered porch in Cape Cod. It was midsummer 2019 in Falmouth, those magical weeks when sparkling, balmy days roll one into the next. I wrote this handbook in a time of complete innocence of what lay ahead for us. A worldwide pandemic that would shut down our universe was a thing of bad movies—ones to which I would definitely give a giant miss! But here I am during the coronavirus shutdown, with oodles of time on my hands, editing this little tome that I basically plonked onto these pages over a year ago. You'll hear me talking about how to be a good houseguest, how to shop in antique stores, and other things that, to be honest, seem positively trivial right now. I certainly hope there are a few antique shops standing when this is all over!

Quick aside to the reader: This isn't your regular "How To" book. This is my view of the world. Take what you like, discard the rest, make it your own if you like. As far as I am concerned, the only rules regarding creativity and the way you live your life is that there are no rules! Make your own rules. Please just listen to the voice that lives inside your brain.

So, after chatting to my lovely team and the family, I decided that it would be hopeless to unpick and alter my words now—I would just be left with a strange pile of nothingness. So please be aware. I know that it seems strange for me to be working on this book now, but my hope is that it will be a siren call for when the good life returns for us all! As Her Majesty, wearing that marvelous green wool frock, told us in her rare coronavirus address to the nation, "We'll meet again!"

Chapter 1

Do you long to become a super stylish and authentic human being? Do you want to live a life that is meaningful, surrounded with things that you love and that echo the true person that nestles inside of you? This is not a money thing. This is a define-your-life thing, and you can choose to be that person!

The number one task for you is to develop "AN EYE," and the only way to do that is to become a "noticer." My children invented this word to describe me; I think they might have used it more as a pejorative when they were naughty teenagers, but not much got by me! They still say my second career should have been as a detective. For example, "Wasn't there $65 in my purse?" or "Why is there 50 percent water in all the clear booze in our bar?" (This after our dinner guests remained surprisingly sober and unjolly!) Those were the days!

Once you get started becoming a noticer, the rest of your stylish life will fall gently into place. I promise!

I suggest you start by noticing the little things—when you're walking in the park, or in the woods, or on the city streets. Accepting where you are is a big part of how becoming a noticer begins within you. As your eye lands on some particular thing, it sends a small signal to your brain that says, "That's cool!" Teach yourself to stop for a moment. What is it that caught your eye? The contours of a building in the evening light? The rough pattern of the patinated bark on a tree? The weary lines chiseled into the face of an old person going about their day? Whatever it is, you need to be ready to start listening, become aware of the signals that your eyes are sending to your brain. You need to allow your brain to file away these data, because they are developing your "eye." Your very own unique eye!

So many people walk through life blind to the mysterious and fascinating world that surrounds them. You can change this! I have often considered why Instagram is having such a wonderful effect on people—besides wanting a lot of Likes! It introduces us to another way of seeing. It helps us become a noticer and be noticed as well. We have a natural tendency to want to charm, amuse, and enlighten our own Instagram audience. Suddenly, people who never really looked before are now on the lookout for the odd, the fun, the unusual, or the perfect light. Instagram is turning people into noticers! It is also connecting like-minded people and opening up our lives to new and exciting circles. This is a good thing!

I find it so interesting that our brains choose certain things to collect and file away. Why does that particular image grab our attention? How does a particular colour make some old memory resurface in our consciousness? What happened in our past that makes us spend a few seconds looking at the face of a stranger or the fabric of the curtains in a window we are passing by?

 By the way, London is my all-time favorite place to wander and stare into windows. English people leave their curtains wide open—so perfect for nosy types like me to peek inside. Don't you think other people's lives are oh so fascinating?

Something I've come to realise, now that I have had the great privilege of spending a considerable amount of time on this earth, is that if you are unhappy or unfulfilled by your daily existence, if you don't feel settled or are anxious about some of the paths that you have chosen for yourself, it is extremely hard, if not almost impossible, to become a good noticer. Dealing with unhappiness and anxiety takes up way too much of your bandwidth. To be a good noticer, you need to start fixing your life. Just small steps in the right direction will do.

Please know, I fully understand that not everyone has the

capacity or wherewithal to fix their life, and that's okay, but you can still push the stress away and make a little bubble of mind space to hold onto something for yourself. When you take back your joy, all the wonders of the world you live in will start presenting themselves to you. I promise!

When I look back on the movie of my life, I realise what a privilege it has been to have lived on three continents, to have traveled to fascinating places, gone to amazing parties, and dined in wonderful locales. However, it saddens me that some of the wonders of that past life were lost on me. Fortunately, plenty of those visual snapshots still managed to get filed away in my brain despite the noise of the rest of the conversations going on in my head. My younger self spent a lot of time worrying about the direction her life was taking and grinding over how to untangle unhappy relationships. That was a long time ago. I am happy to say that I found the courage to fix things. Having a mother who always told me that I was funny and pretty and interesting made me understand that I didn't have to listen to the negative noise, jabs, and stories—

my JOURNEY is part of WHO I AM

ENGLAND

SOUTH Africa

TAKE
BACK
YOUR
JOY

I could break free from them. It wasn't easy, it was a little messy, but since then my creative inner life has blossomed.

I hope this helps people to reach inside themselves and find their source of hope and courage or the person that truly sees you. And take that to the bank and deposit it there!

I wouldn't dream of rewinding my life. My journey is part of me. The obstacles became my gifts. I accept my complicated life journey wholeheartedly! It made me who I am today, resilient and enthusiastic, and I accept the worldview it has gifted me.

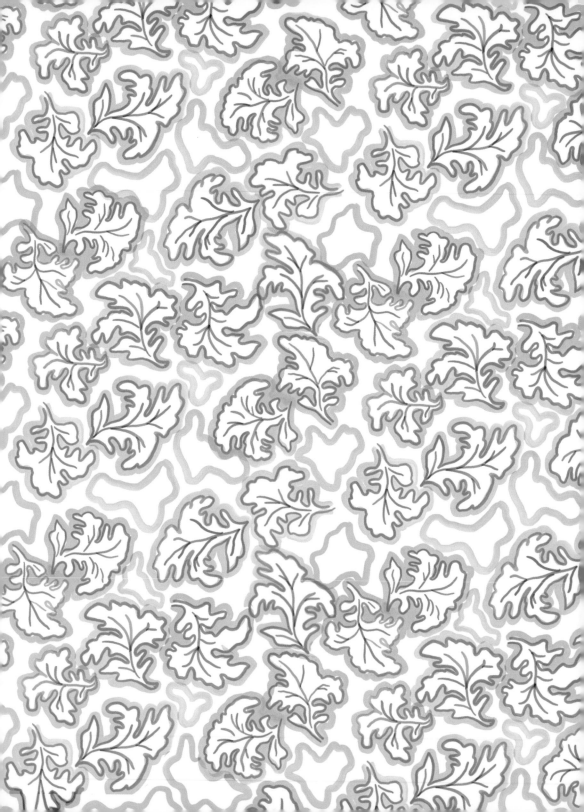

HOW TO CONQUER JUNK STORES

Chapter 2

So now that you're working on being a noticer and working on having a happy life, it's time to talk about one of my favourite pastimes: the joy of the hunt in junk stores, or vintage stores, or antique emporiums. Your house will love you for it! Lots of people find the whole experience of stepping into one of these establishments brimming with dreary talcum-powder-smelling granny stuff, bad amateur art, and—heaven forbid—blobby brown amateur pottery, totally overwhelming. And who can blame them? But wait! There is an art to the perfect find.

My first hint is don't try too hard. It's like golf, the harder you try, the more a good outcome will elude you; it's frustrating, I know!

I like to put myself into a kind of a trance, and wander along, letting my eye flit over the array of weird goods in my path. When I see something that seizes my attention and has that *je ne sais quoi,* I stop, pick it up, and see how it feels in my hands. And then there's the price tag to examine. Over time, you will develop a sort of cash register in your brain. You find an object that charms you, say, a little lustre jug. Lustre is an adorable type of shimmery nineteenth-century ceramic, usually pink or coppery in colour. I went through a couple of years of serious lustre lust! Also, I am a complete sucker for an adorable little jug!

 Why I love jugs: Jugs have so many uses, and I love the shape of them. They hint of hospitality and comfort and welcome! I love vintage cut glass ones filled with water on your lunch table. They are just perfect for a little bunch of flowers placed on the bedside table of your guest bedroom, but more about guest bedrooms later! I love them lined up on a shelf. I love mixing vintages and patterns—striped and splattered and flowery.

an ADORABLE, LITTLE Jug

When junking, the next most important thing to consider is the price the dealer is asking. At this point, that little lustre jug will either come home with you or not. It is most important that the price the dealer is asking is within range of what your internal cash register tells you is a reasonable price; it takes some time, but you will soon develop this instinct. So in this case, it should probably be about $35 if it's fabulous, or less if it's a bit of a meh. The find needs to feel like something of a bargain; otherwise, it's no fun! The price of this jug has little to do with how much cash you have in your wallet. The find has everything to do with whether your purchase is a wonderful little coup, and you walk away with your brown paper parcel thinking you did rather nicely, thank you! You absolutely need to stick to these rules of junk store buying! A greedy dealer duping the unsuspecting and uneducated public really is not good! Eventually, all these pleasant hours whiled away trawling through dusty places will become a sort of meditation for you. It certainly is for me! And your house will be layered with wonderfully random objects that appeal completely to your sensibility. Best of all, your home will start to feel like a real person lives there! And that person could only be YOU!

There are no other rules in rummaging—just the ones I mentioned! I say this particularly for my friends and neighbors here in the northeast of America. Yes, in some aspects of life, too much education can be a not-so-good thing! There is no right or wrong to what takes your fancy. No one will be grading you on what you found, fell madly in love with, and brought home with you to put on your bookshelf or mantlepiece.

You cannot get an A, so please just give up on that idea! Listen to your heart and buy the damn thing, however odd or unexpected. Oh, and please don't buy what you think your bestie will think is cool; that is never cool. Listen to your own inner designer voice and become the unapologetic noticer you really are!

When you're ready to take the next leap, and your usual round of local antiquing spots no longer intimidates you, it's time to take it to the next level! Bring a bunch of like-minded friends (it's very important to avoid having any whiners in your group) and try one of the big antique markets—if only for the people watching! The antique dealer group is a fascinating slice of our subculture. Sometimes it's all I can do to keep my jaw from hitting the floor! The outfits, the seventies hair, the tattoos, the liberal number of missing teeth—but a friendlier crowd you will not find. You must go and see for yourself.

The sprawling Brimfield Antique Flea Market is close to where I live, so I go there from time to time with a group of good friends. It is either ungodly hot or arctic cold, so do not get caught with the wrong attire. About shoes, wearing only the most worn-in and comfortable will do! Brimfield is a perfect example of the casual and informal down market antiquing foray.

If Brimfield's style is a bit down market, the other end of the spectrum is London with its upmarket brocante shows. When I lived in London, I loved the brocante shows that happened from time to time in the Chelsea or Kensington town halls. The best ever is the Decorative Antiques and Textiles Fair in Battersea Park! I can sometimes catch it if it coincides with Decorex and London Design Week. The timing is always a bit random in a British sort of way. This fair is my all-time favourite antique show—the wares are very close to my taste, and it's oh so civilised.

THE STORY of my MANTEL

Tourist Shops

John Derian Splurge

Old Sandwich Gla[ss]
one of my obsession[s]

BRIMFIELD Antique FLEA · MARKET

When in London I stay with my darling daughter, Jessica, who gets dragged along with me. She is a great noticer and has developed an excellent eye over the years.

About children: If children aren't a part of your life, or if you choose not to have them, please do not let this mar your experience in any way. There is not just one way to live a fulfilled life. This is your life, and it is uniquely yours!

Whether you're at the Decorative Antiques and Textiles Fair, or Decorex, which is part of the annual London Design Week, the ladies of London are always dressed in their tasteful best. I love the getup of the ladies that have just come in from the country wearing their tweed capes over their elegant cashmere twinsets, or the Chanel-from-tip-to-toe London third wives with their flamboyant decorator friend on their arm.

At these marvelous events, the champagne bar in the center of things is buzzing right from opening time. Champagne is always a good idea! There's unfailingly a lovely place to eat your lunch, usually in some marvelously disguised tent. The atmosphere is so very merry, and everyone has a nice glass of lunchtime wine with their salad—*quelle horreur!*

This is not the Brimfield crowd, but that's not to say that both are not equally delightful in their own way. At the Decorative Antiques and Textiles Fair, every stall is utterly droolworthy, but sadly most of the treasures are priced right out of my reach. You can see the heavyweights wheeling and dealing behind the scenes. It's fascinating. Even so, it's so good for your eye to go and look, soak it all up, and admire the dazzling array of tasteful furniture, art, and objects.

Your job is to form an opinion, then decide what you would buy and bring home with you. This process will translate into the treasures that you find down the road in the dusty little antique store and that you will bring home and tell the world, "I bought this because I liked it!" There will be no mistaking that this is your home, not a page from a magazine. It is a space most specifically yours!

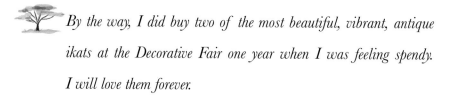 *By the way, I did buy two of the most beautiful, vibrant, antique ikats at the Decorative Fair one year when I was feeling spendy. I will love them forever.*

Finally, for an over-the-top market, Round Top Antiques Fair in Round Top, Texas, is mind-blowing! It is huge, and very Texan! It's probably best to get a well-informed friend to help you or do some good online research before you go. It's a must to find the right farms to go to and to know which to give a giant miss! I was taken to Marburger Farm at Round Top by my friend and Texan designer extraordinaire, Meredith Ellis. It was an incredible experience—dealers from all over the world, and the heat, and the makeup, and the cowboy boots, and the huge hair! Yikes, I loved every bit of it, except for the lunch, which was barbeque on a slab of white bread roll and goopy coleslaw, sitting on a bench in a hot tent. There are times when you feel like you're in another universe. I looked around, and even the billionaire ladies, with their interior designer entourages in tow, were chomping it all down—an acquired taste, I assume!

Small town or big city, flea markets are an absolutely fun way to train your noticing eye! Over time, you might find you develop a taste for a certain thing. You might become obsessed with a certain colour or a certain vintage of a thing, and then you start to look for these particular things in your junk store forays. Suddenly, you're a collector, and even though being a collector is not so fashionable these days, who cares! Collecting is a wonderful hobby—above all, it is utterly yours. My taste for the things I collect ebbs and flows, but I seldom purge or toss things out. You never know when you might fall back in love with oyster plates, or Cumberland, or whatever.

HOW TO HAVE OVERNIGHT GUESTS

(Without having a nervous breakdown and with everyone staying friends)

Chapter 3

Staying with friends is quite an emotional commitment. You are a kind of prisoner in their home, and it's easy to feel a little trapped by the vagaries of your host's household and their idiosyncratic ways. When you stay overnight with friends or family, you are surrendering your independence (which is very hard for single-minded and A-type personalities); that's quite a lot to surrender.

Some articles in books and magazines recommend that you spend the night in your own guest room with the express purpose of finding out if there are any uncomfortable little niggles about the room that might drive your overnight guests crazy! I believe there is no real need for the actual special guest room stay-over, because most of us have voluntarily slept in our own guest rooms once or twice. Remember when you had that nasty cold, or even worse, your bedroom partner had a nasty cold? Don't forget the middle of the night, I-honestly-don't-know-how-I-ever-could-have-married-you! moment, but the last thing you are thinking about then is the quality of the bed linen!

Here are my key guest room pointers:

- Your guest room should be super, super clean! Nothing is more upsetting than the random strand of hair lurking in the bathroom.
- A nice comfortable mattress that has been bought in the present century is essential.
- I like my bed made up with clean crisp sheets, a single blanket, and a duvet to pull over the bed for chilly nights. Of course, this is just the way I like to do it; everyone has their own preference. An extra blanket in the cupboard for people that have come from warmer climates is important. My South African family are always shocked

by how cold it is in New England, even in the shoulder seasons, and they want to pile on the bedding!

- There's nothing lovelier than goose down pillows, lots of them. Sinking into a goose down puff at the end of a busy day is heavenly.

- A bottle of mineral water and drinking glasses for next to the bed is an essential touch.

- A good hairdryer in the bathroom that really works is important. Also, it needs to be near a mirror.

- Curtains or shades that darken the room are an essential little luxury, and it really helps for light sleepers. This is especially important for people who have traveled from different time zones (jet lag is such a killer) and I find it is exacerbated in an unfamiliar environment!

- Make sure you have some nice soap, shampoo, and conditioner in the bathroom, and moisturizer, of course. Oh, and a couple extra rolls of loo paper are very, very important!

- I love to put a little fresh posy in an old jug or vintage vase on the dressing table or next to the bed. It doesn't

have to be fancy. A sprig from the garden, or supermarket flowers when well chosen, are perfectly fine. Flowers say, "You're welcome, you're expected. I went to this extra bit of trouble for you." It's a nice message to your guests.

The most important five minutes of the stay are when your guests arrive. Look happy to see them! People like to be fussed over a bit. Offer them tea, coffee, a drink, whatever seems appropriate.

My hubbie always shows our guests the bar and where the tea and coffee are kept. He urges them to help themselves whenever they like, to whatever they like. "There's absolutely no need to ask," he insists. People love that! It puts them instantly at ease, though they still tend to ask.

Lastly, remember how you felt when you were a houseguest, and prepare to meet those needs for your guests. There is nothing worse than feeling starving hungry in someone else's house and knowing that dinner is hours away.

A quick aside: I borrowed an idea from a friend we stayed with in Florida. She kept a bunch of nibbles out on her kitchen island for when we were passing by—a bowl of fruit, a basket of cookies, maybe a few containers of almonds or cashews. It felt so welcoming.

I think the hungriest I have ever been in my life was at an English country shooting party in a big old rattling pile of a house. It was miserable grey weather outside, and we were being casually informed that the cook from the village was going to be a bit late due to a family emergency. What? Let me just gnaw my arm off in front of this miserable spluttering fire right now! Some English people prefer their dogs and their gin to their food, be warned. Maybe pack a granola bar or two in your overnight bag if the occasion arises!

The next important thing is to tell your guests the plans for the day. They would probably like to know if you're staying in or going out for dinner. Tell them what time you expect them up in the morning or whether they can feel free to sleep in. You should already have alerted them if they needed to pack any special clothes for things they'll be doing during their stay. Women especially hate it when a nice occasion is sprung on them by their hosts and their perfect outfit is at home hanging in their cupboard.

To be on the safe side, I always put something pretty at the bottom of my suitcase. A just-in-case dress can save you from a horrible moment of having to wear boring old jeans to last-minute supper at the neighbors'. The outfit can just stay in the suitcase if you don't need it.

So, that about covers it. Be nice. Let your guests help with meal prep in the kitchen if they insist. I prefer to go it alone or have a daughter or two help me out, but let your guests feel included. If they want to be involved in the kitchen fray, so be it.

And by the way, try not to dash over with a coaster every time they put down their drink. So not cool! English people are the best at being super laid back about having people stay in their houses. They never fuss over spills, or minor breakages, or dogs on the furniture, or newspapers all over the floor. I love them for that.

HOW TO BE A GOOD GUEST

(And be invited back)

Chapter 4

The aforementioned rules for hosts should be applied to yourself as a guest. Ask questions. Try to be helpful, but stay away if they really don't want you in the kitchen. Always bring a thoughtful gift. If it's booze, don't suggest opening and drinking it immediately because you are dying to try that vintage! My mother hates it when she has people to stay and they trail around behind her all day long. It brings out the bitchy in her! So please make sure you have a good book, your iPad or a pile of magazines you need to go through. Keep yourself amused until you are needed.

HOW TO HAVE A FUN DINNER PARTY

(That even you enjoy)

Chapter 5

Dinner parties are hard. First you have to get your head around that, then you can decide if you really want to go ahead and do it. Then plunge in. Dinner parties require your full commitment, but they sure can be wonderful! It's sort of like putting on a play in your dining room.

You're probably aware of this, but people don't really have old-fashioned, grown-up dinner parties much anymore. They are very difficult to pull off successfully. One of the key ingredients is having a nice mix of people. Have you tried recently to get a nice mix of people who are all available on a Friday or a Saturday night without having to put it on their calendars a year in advance? In this day and age, people are so busy. They move around a lot. So gathering that perfect balance of guests required for a memorable dinner party is now increasingly challenging.

Here are my dinner party pointers:

Squeeze in! Fit as many people around your table as you can. People love a squeeze! It feels festive. Drag in your kitchen chairs, nobody cares!

Keep the food delish and abundant! Cook things you know how to cook. Regular food that you cook for your family is perfectly fine.

A little history: When I was in my newlywed twenties—in another country, another husband, and another life—I took some cooking classes (it's what nice newlywed Johannesburg girls did) and started getting a little competitive with the other girls in our friend group. I was always trying to be just that little bit fancier, so I decided to attempt quenelle (little poached balls of egg white and flaked fish) as my knock-their-socks-off course! Everyone was seated expectantly at my immaculately set table. (We were so serious when we were young ladies playing grown-up.) I excused myself and dropped the first batch into the gently simmering water waiting on the stove, and… Mush! It totally dissolved into a nasty, foamy mess. But I persevered—I'm a Capricorn woman, I persevere! Next batch, fresh water, same mush. Oh, the shame I felt as I went back to the sitting room to announce that the first course had been cancelled due to lack of skill! I was mortified—Capricorn again! Let this be a lesson to all of us, dinner parties are not the right time to expand your cooking repertoire.

Present a bountiful table! Your party needs to look like you over-catered, badly! There is nothing worse than "democratic

SHOP up a STORM

potatoes," which is another of my mum's "worst hosting" pet peeves—that is, one man, one potato. There is nothing happy or relaxing about standing at a help-yourself buffet calculating, "If I take two of these very small lamb chops, is that enough for everyone to have two?" You then start silently counting heads and lamb chops. If you're going to drag a bunch of people over to your house on a valuable Friday or Saturday night, shop up a storm and let them see it. When people see a feast, it makes them feel like they're at a fabulous, fun occasion, and they immediately start having a jolly good old time! If you don't want to do this, don't bother having a real dinner party,

just have Sunday night supper in the kitchen, which is actually also just fine.

Let the work begin: plan, plan, PLAN! The thing about effortless entertaining is that it is totally not effortless! Only your guests believe that it all just happened with fairy dust and magic. "Effortless" takes planning ahead and being prepared for any eventuality. Plan Bs are essential, especially when doing an outdoor party: "But Dark Sky said it was only going to start raining at midnight!" Don't rely on apps; been there, done that, and cried upstairs in my bathroom with my very confused doggies, praying to the Universe that she would miraculously scoop up all my dripping guests and pop them back home in their beds!

Take your time! Spread out your dinner party duties over the week before the big date. Make lists if you must. I like to keep my lists in my head; I think making lists in your brain is good for keeping the old muscle flexible. Anyway, just do what you have to do listwise! If you chip away at it and do a little every day, *voila,* it'll all be done, and you'll be ready and cool as a cucumber when showtime arrives. Sliding in my favourite quote from our great, and dearly missed, Nelson Mandela: "It always seems impossible until it's done." That resonates with me just about once a day!

This is vaguely how my dinner party run-up timeline works:

A week before: Shoot out a quick text to your guests confirming date and time and any other important details— it's good to know everyone is in the country and there won't be gaps at the table that make the people mix unbalanced.

Quick confession: I never feel nervous about the food or the general preparations, but a couple of days before, I start to convince myself that no one will turn up! Who knows what awful thing must have happened in my childhood to give me the fear of no one coming to my party. I'm working on it.

IT ALWAYS SEEMS IMPOSSIBLE UNTIL IT'S DONE

- Nelson Mandela

Five days before: Get the booze sorted; it's bulky and heavy and requires its own shopping trip.

Four days before: Buy all the ingredients you need that won't go off—nuts, olives, tinned things, frozen things, pasta, rice, you get the drift.

Three days before: Go to the flower market or wherever you get your flowers and find some really nice-looking and super-fresh flowers. The supermarket flowers are fine, by the way; just buy an abundance of them, and don't get the chrysanthemums (they remind me of gas station flowers). Buying your flowers early gives them time to open and release some of their delish scent into your house.

Two days before: Buy all the perishable items such as salad ingredients, veggies, or cheese. Remember, if you're going to need avocados, buy them now. It is amazing how the dinner party gods will remove every nice soft avocado from every one of your usual haunts when you are in a dinner party panic.

On another note, stone fruit and tomatoes should go onto the kitchen counter to keep ripening and make lots of lovely, tasty sugar for when you need them. I really hate food straight from the fridge! Tasteless!

On the day before: Set your table. Give your glasses a good wipe. I like to make my table look really festive. Dig around for different containers that you have in your house, no matter how odd, and fill them with your opened flowers. (There's a little chapter on flowers coming up.) Mix up your china patterns, your friends will not expect everything to match. I love coloured water glasses as another layer of bling. You can find cheap and cheerful vintage ones in that local antique store/junk store that you are now totally familiar with!

If you feel like splurging, Anthropologie has an everchanging tabletop section that never disappoints. They also have lovely printed linen napkins, which are a must! I also have found some good napkins on the Pottery Barn sale—they are always having some kind of special offer. More colour for your table, yay! You might not realise it, but investment in these things will make you happy forever. I bought some napkins in Nice in the airport shop many decades ago, and when I bring them out, it's a mini trip down memory lane. Yup, life's a journey!

At this point, it is a good idea to set up your bar (excluding all the things that need to be chilled). Having a nicely set up bar—with good openers, sliced lemons and limes, and with everything in full view for your guests to help themselves—will take so much pressure off you. I find that guests feel immediately relaxed with something important to do—like make drinks. It also keeps them out of the kitchen! This sets the happy tone you want to create, super relaxed, but super organised! An unrelaxed host equals very unrelaxed guests! If you're feeling spendy, a bar cart is a wonderful thing! You used to be able to pick them up for a song on eBay before our dear millennials Instagrammed the heck out of them, but Target or Wayfair may carry some good, inexpensive ones. Later, you can find new uses for it, like piling it with indoor plants, or using it as somewhere to drop your keys when you come in the front door—that is, if you don't want to have your booze out all the time (teenagers)!

The big day! On the big day of your do, get all the chopping, browning, and general heavy lifting of the cooking done in the morning. Take the whole meal to the point where it would spoil if you did the steps any closer to the time of your party.

Now take a walk, relax, read your book, or lie in the bathtub (my favourite take-it-down-a-notch method). Don't put on your nice clean clothes until you have taken care of the last-minute dirty things (I've made this mistake before), like quickly mopping the kitchen floor or bringing in firewood. Oh, empty your dishwasher so it's ready to receive all the used dinner party detritus. You see, now all you need to do is have a good time—totally composed and smiling—and pretend it was all nothing!

In other countries it is considered rude to arrive exactly on time, and giving your host a good fifteen-minute panic cushion is regarded as good form. But that's not always true in certain regions here in the United States, as I discovered in my early days! Being dead on time is considered a courtesy in New England, but in my opinion, guests who arrive even two minutes early should be garroted. Never, ever do that to anyone!

Finally, the last thing you want is to be an exhausted heap when the doorbell rings, because this is your rodeo and you

need to be on! I have been to many a party that goes totally flat because, after getting everyone into their lair, the host, thinking that their work is done, withdraws to the corner of the room to chat quietly to their bestie! Wrong! This is how English hosts shine—they are expert introducers! First, they dig around in their head for something interesting and mutually interesting to both parties, then they find a complimentary way to bracket it in their introduction. Let me demonstrate: "Mally, this is Mike. Didn't I hear you say that you have played golf at Green Acres golf course down at the Cape? Aren't you and hubbie members there?" And now we're off to the races!

MY
PARTY
TIPS

Chapter 6

If it's an important occasion and the caterers have been called in, there is no need for the party to feel stiff and corporate. I always like to do my own table, or at least work with the florist so that the flowers look like I did them! Also, I like to use as many of my own serving dishes as I can, so it still looks like a party at my house, but with more organised and slightly more professional food. I always mention to the catering manager that we like to keep things casual in our house. Obsequious service is just so uncool.

If you're doing a big stand-up-and-yack party, avoid the endless trays of itty-bitty bites of hors d'oeuvres that never seem to leave you totally satisfied. And the work! Nuts, olives, some hummus, and veggies are perfect to get started, and then I like to do a couple of large dishes of something delicious and hot with an accompanying salad and lots of artisan bread.

Bobotie is a South African party favourite that I often serve. My recipe for Bobotie came from my mum. It is borrowed from the cuisine of the Malay community that settled in Cape Town many years ago. The patchwork quilt of food in South Africa is a thing of amazement—you will find that out if you visit! Bobotie is served with a bunch of accompanying sambals—little bowls of chutney, chopped

tomatoes, bananas in yoghurt, cucumber salad, and on and on. Heaping your plate with all these flavors and textures makes for a very happy atmosphere. This is a meal that makes it possible for people to perch wherever, with just a single plate to juggle. In addition, I always do a huge green salad for the inevitable calorie counters!

This recipe has been handed over and adapted umpteen times. I have no ownership, so do what you like with it and enjoy!

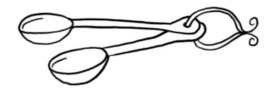

Emmie's Bobotie

2 large onions, diced
2 cloves garlic, chopped
vegetable oil
butter
2 lbs. minced beef
2 Tbsp. regular curry powder
2 Tbsp. apricot jam
2 Tbsp. chutney (You can buy Major Grey's in most
       supermarkets or buy the original Mrs. Balls—
       I kid you not—off Amazon.)
2 Tbsp. raisins
2 slices of white bread soaked in milk
2 eggs plus a cup more of milk
Salt and pepper

Sweat 2 large onions and 2 cloves of garlic, chopped, in a little vegetable oil and big chunk of butter. Next, add the curry powder to the onions and garlic, then brown the meat in the same pot. Add the apricot jam, chutney, raisins, and mushy bread. Season to taste. Cook on the stovetop until meat is done through. Place in a Pyrex dish and cover with 2 eggs mixed with half a cup of milk (this creates the golden-brown crust). Cook in a moderate oven, about 350°F, until golden brown and set on top.

Serve with traditional sambals (side dishes): diced onion, green pepper and tomato, dried coconut, sliced banana (keep from browning with lemon juice), sliced cucumber with yoghurt, and more chutney. Serve on turmeric yellow rice with raisins. (Add ¼ teaspoon of turmeric into the Basmati rice while it's cooking, then throw in a handful of seedless raisins right at the end.) Your guests will love it. (Note: I have made it with fake minced meat for my veggie daughter and it is actually quite good.)

EMMIE'S
BOBOTIE

2 onions

clove of garlic

Salt

pepper

curry

Some Butter

Eggs

white bread

cup of milk

vegetable oil

Chutney + apricot jam

2 lbs minced meat

tbsp of raisins

SIDE DISHES:
~ diced veg

~ cucumber + yoghurt

~ dried coconut

Though I love my South African Malay recipes, summer seems to bring out my love for all things Italian!

My favourite party plan is to do a help-yourself *alfresco* Italian table. I like my Italian table to be groaning with salami, avocados, burrata, mozzarella with tons of chopped basil (best smell in the world), deep red tomatoes soaked in good balsamic vinegar (nice and thick and sweet, not bitter), and lashings of good olive oil. Add to that a huge plate crammed with prosciutto with figs or melon; the figs at the end of the summer are spectacular. At the end of the table, I place a giant salad with plenty of arugula and a wooden board with lots of crunchy bread. There's nothing nicer than pretending you're having lunch in the Campo in Siena! The effect that abundance has on your guests is amazing. The atmosphere will immediately become festive if you've put an effort into your entertaining, and your guests will feel the love, I guarantee it!

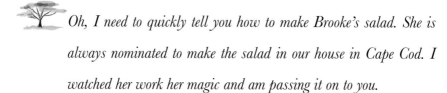 *Oh, I need to quickly tell you how to make Brooke's salad. She is always nominated to make the salad in our house in Cape Cod. I watched her work her magic and am passing it on to you.*

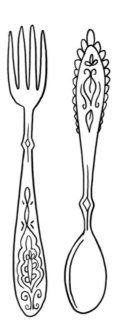

Brooke's Salad

Finely chop one large or two small garlic cloves and toss in a big wooden salad bowl.

Tear up your greens and place them in the bowl on top of the garlic.

Chop up the tomatoes.

Add any or all of the following:

> Cubed cucumber
>
> Red, green, or yellow peppers
>
> Raw asparagus, chopped
>
> Raw corn off the cob
>
> Fresh mangetout peas
>
> Endive, sliced
>
> Green onions or thinly sliced red onion
>
> Anything else you find at the green grocer that looks delicious and in season

Add one or two ripe avocados, cubed.

Squeeze the juice of one large or two small lemons over everything.

Add a large pinch of sea salt. (I love Maldon Salt, which is available on Amazon or in good supermarkets. Not too salty, just right!)

Add some good grinds of black pepper and a huge glug of good olive oil right over the top.

Mix well.

OMG Yum! Honestly, none will come back to the kitchen!

THE JOY OF FLOWERS IN YOUR HOUSE

(And what my mother taught me)

Chapter 7

My mum taught me to love flowers. When my sister and I were little, she would always go out into the garden and add a flower sprig to go under the ribbon of the gifts we took to birthday parties. Without thinking, I added a sprig to a hostess gift I was wrapping the other day, and the memories came flooding back.

My mother's love of gardens and flowers has flowed into all my siblings. I know it's not always easy to have living things surrounding you, but I never resort to fake; I just don't see the point. Dusty fake flowers or plants make me feel depressed.

But I love some fakes like tole flowers or the paper geraniums made by The Green Vase. (Tole flowers are generally made of metal or tin. The French word *tole* literally means enameled or lacquered metalware, painted and sometimes gilded, but not necessarily.) Now those are chic to die for! I know it's an expense and hard work to keep plants and flowers in your house, but I love the way it invites nature into your habitat. It reminds us that we are just a small part of the many living organisms that make up our universe. When you look intensely into a flower, you are looking into the face of the whole miracle of life on earth. Well, that's my view anyway. Some people feel that way when they sail on the ocean or sit in a roaring sports stadium. To each his own.

Just like when browsing in a junk shop, the trick to flowers is, once again, not to try too hard. Over time you will discover, through experimentation, which flowers last the best, which flowers give you the most joy, and which containers make for the most attractive arrangements. I am always trying different things; there is no wrong way to enjoy flowers.

More about flowers: The English do mighty floral arrangements like no one else! They have an artful way with flowers that is so grand yet tender; it really demonstrates their love of nature and their gardens. Even a single sprig of a wildflower, picked on your walk and put in a tiny vase—a champagne flute will do—placed next to the sink or on your desk as you work, is inspiring. It might only last a couple of hours but brings such joy to the eye! From a single stem to the mighty arrangements you see on the reception tables of fancy hotels, fresh flowers are always right!

If someone sends you flowers from a florist or brings them to your house as a hostess gift, always keep the vases because they are so useful. I sometimes use one of these large, squat glass vases in my ridiculous collection (accumulated over many, many years) as an extra ice bucket, for fruit salad, or scattered down the dining room table, each one jammed with a different type or colour of flower. I then intersperse the vases with votives and sometimes little growing plants in terra-cotta pots. All these containers of flowers crammed down the middle of the table makes it look like a wildly beautiful garden is growing right there. I love doing this especially in the spring in New England. It's fun to jump the gun and fill your dinner party table with a garden of tulips and daffodils that you can find in the early spring supermarket. After a long cold winter, hope springs eternal, and a spring garden down your table when the leaves haven't even burst yet makes people smile.

By the way, I am aware that being a person who collects stuff, like vases and votives, has gotten a bad rap of late. Everyone likes to say how light they feel when they get rid of everything they haven't used in the last six months. But tell me, how many times have you needed just that thing right after it went into last week's trash? I understand that mine is presently an unfashionable point of view, but if you have the room, keep your things; don't go out and buy more stuff. Think of the environment; every time you repurpose something, you are saving the world from another piece of trash that goes into our landfills. Buying vintage and repurposing are the ultimate recycling!

HOW TO LOVE YOUR HOUSE

Chapter 8

If we are honest, learning to love and share your house (and table) takes time. So does learning to love ourselves. It takes openness. Not everyone feels the need to love and share their house, and that's okay. For some people, their house is just a part of how their life functions—where they eat, sleep, and watch TV—and that's perfectly okay. That's their choice and I respect it.

But so often I hear people grumble that they don't love their house enough to open its doors and share it freely with dinner guests. They tell me they don't have good taste. "Good taste" is not just one thing! It is totally subjective. Your house

and the way you choose to entertain guests needs to be good taste through your lens, and that is all that is important. Good taste isn't something you just wake up with! Your taste is a culmination of all your life experiences—the places you have lived, worked, traveled—and all these images sponged up in your brain. No worries! There are always ways of improving your style, of getting closer to what you really like, and you can do this in a number of ways. You can read design books, blogs and magazines, but those usually show very rarified interiors that actually just make me feel exhausted to look at them! They are totally inaccessible and often over-tweaked, not my vibe at all! I would simply say, "Be bold, be real, be yourself, and be happy" and you, your house, and your guests will love you for it! Trust me on this one!

MALLY'S FAVORITES

John Robshaw for napkins and placemats

Ubuntu Life for great gifts

Goodee for ethically sourced gifts

Emma Bridgwater for nicest everyday plates

Fresh is a wonderful brand for soaps

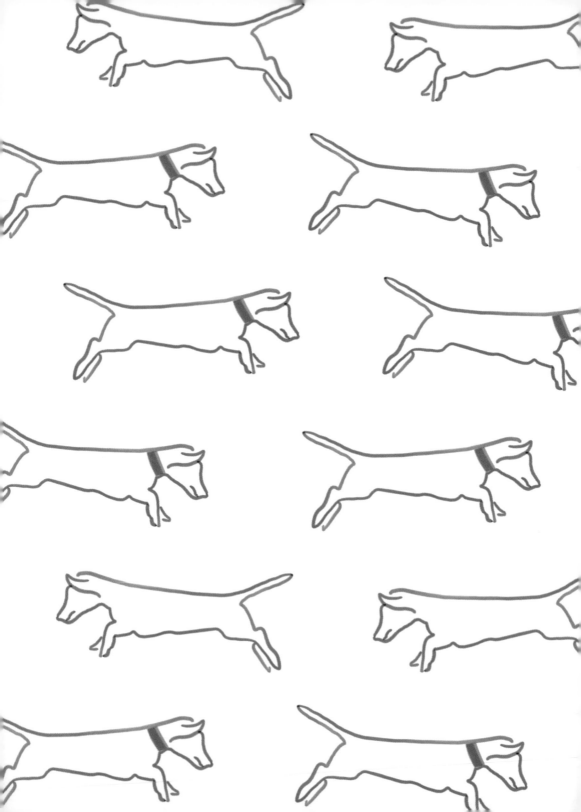

I'LL
LEAVE
YOU
WITH
THIS

Chapter 9

First, having become a successful noticer, enroll yourself in the there's-no-time-like-the-present club. Those ideas, that adorable bowl in the junk store, that burst of enthusiasm to make a start on something new—they all float away with time! Don't think that ideas hang around and wait for you to catch up—you need to grab each and every moment and opportunity. Oh yes, and don't forget to add the most vital ingredient: the dreaded follow-through! It's all a waste of time unless you stop procrastinating and just get on with it. Putting things off to a more appropriate time is just a subtle way of limiting yourself. A very good friend once told me not to "self-limit"! At first, I didn't get what he was saying to me; it took a while to sink in, but then I got it. We are all guilty of inventing excuses. Telling ourselves that it's really not the right time, that we're too busy, that it's not that good of an idea after all, that people will think we're weird or presumptuous…. All of these so-called reasons are the very definition of self-limiting! Sometimes persistence supersedes either brains or talent.

Second, find your enthusiasm button and use it! Being too cool for school is actually nauseating. My dear mother used to shout, "Be enthusiastic!" as we ran out of the house to go to a party. I thought she was being silly, but now I get it!

Don't worry if people look at you like you're a little crazy! I have built myself a nice shield to ward off those looks! If something charms you, why not show it? Being self-conscious is a silly habit that you need to break!

So, if you like something or are really enjoying something, please don't keep it to yourself, and certainly don't self-limit; just show it! Enthusiasm is infectious! When you show your enthusiasm, you give those around you permission to do the same! Surely, the world could do with a whole load of your good vibes right now!

Afterword

Mally Skok, my dear friend, is a force of nature, style queen, designer, creator, and born hostess. Most importantly, Mally is a life enhancer. You feel alive after spending time with her because her whole being radiates a generosity of spirit and she is such fun. It shows in everything she does and creates.

Mally is one of the most hospitable people I've ever known, and she wants you to have fun at her gorgeous, warmly layered, and interesting house. It all starts with the details she talks about in this charming book. It's her philosophy of life. Mally takes her readers along as she shows us how her philosophy plays out in decorating, friendship, and being a resolved human being. When entertaining, she makes her home a place you want to be in. Her house is a place you get excited to visit. It is filled with such fun, laughter, delicious food, and diverse and interesting people. Her house tells the story of who she is—colourful, open-hearted, inclusive, and generous. She is a designer with an incredible eye for textiles, colour, and objects that have meaning and add emotional resonance to the room. Filled with a love of life and unbounded enthusiasm, this little book is a dose of pure Mally!

Serena Crawford
Plettenberg Bay, South Africa

FIREPOND

PRESS